A DIFFERENT KIND OF GRIEF

WHEN ETERNAL HOPE IS UNSURE

EMMIE SEALS

CONTENTS

SPECIAL NOTE

Throughout this book you'll see my illustrations of hydrangeas. If you find yourself needing a break to clear your mind or process, feel free to color them in while you do so.

INTRODUCTION

DEAR READER,

First, let me say that I am so sorry for your loss. I assume that if you have picked up this book, you are hoping to read something written within these pages which will help to calm the raging storm inside. The anger. The pain. The confusion. The uncertainty. You may feel like you are sinking and shifting through sand. You may feel what I have felt: *I cannot do this alone. I need help to get through this.*

I am writing to fellow brothers and sisters in Christ. If you are not a follower of Jesus, I absolutely welcome your presence here! And I pray that the Lord graciously provides you comfort and a safe place to weep within these pages. Grief impacts all of us in life. For those of us in Christ, there is hope - because our God is in control. He holds all things together. He is good, always. He is with us. He cares for us. He is near to the broken hearted. He is making all things new.

But, where is the hope when the one we lost...may be lost forever?

We believe the Truth that knowing Jesus is all that matters. Having a relationship with Him. Being saved by Him. When we know that He is our salvation and that our hope is sure. How can we look forward to Heaven and eternity with our Savior when our loved one may not be there? How can a place be good, with no pain, and how can every tear be wiped from our eyes, if those we love who died before are not there to welcome us Home?

I will not pretend to have all of the answers.

I am simply a woman impacted by such grief that I felt as though my foundation in Christ was crumbling. I was in a place where I echoed the words of the father in Mark 9:24 continually. "I believe! Help my unbelief." How I understood what he was pleading! How in my deep mourning, I understood how the disciple Paul could write he would give his salvation to save others! (Romans 9:3)

This is my story, and I long for the Lord to use it for His glory. This is the Lord holding me fast. This is the Father proving to me that though I could not see Him, or feel Him, or open His Word, or pray to Him, or have the strength to lift my voice in song, He held me fast.

And this is my letter to you - or rather, my many letters meant for you to take in as you are able.

This night is long. But you, Sweet Sibling in the Lord, will not lose your footing. Our God has you placed upon the Rock and He will be your strength through this storm. You may not be able to hold on. You don't need to. He is able.

FIRST LETTER

WORDS RECEIVED FROM FRIENDS

IT WAS NOT SUPPOSED to be like this. A phone call from my mother while heading out the door to pick up my children from school.

Since I was a little girl, I had prayed with urgency for the salvation of my loved one. I had this desire from a young age to pray for friends on the playground that didn't know Jesus. I wanted to talk to people about Jesus. I was drawn to stories of people traveling to far away lands to share about Jesus. Jim Elliott was an absolute inspiration to me. If he could risk his life for the sake of the gospel, I could risk my next conversation.

And when I would open my mouth to speak to my loved one about Jesus, I'd be told to hush.

And when I would say I was praying for her regarding anything, I'd be told to use my prayers on someone else.

The response was continually, "I'm good." And, "I don't need your prayers."

"I don't want to talk about that."

As in any story, there are multiple perspectives. People see things differently. They experience interactions with individuals differently. We all know this. My relationship with you is completely different than your relationship with your best friend. And your relationship with your best friend will be different than the relationship you had with your first grade teacher.

No matter our relationship with the griever, we all say something similar to those in mourning.

Your (fill in the blank) was such a wonderful person.
She changed my life.
He was the only one who truly got me.
You'll see her again one day.
I never got to say goodbye.
She didn't know how much I loved her.
He didn't know how much I needed him.
She was ready to go.
You'll see him again one day.
I remember the first day I saw her.
It's going to be okay.
He lived a wonderful life.
May she rest in peace.
He is in Heaven.
You'll be reunited again one day.

Your loved one may have recently passed. You may be

preparing yourself to attend a funeral, knowing full well that you will need to hold your tongue - to receive the many sympathies and words of comfort offered, trying to do so with a smile on your face. Trying to receive them well. Graciously. Trying to not be a blubbering spectacle. Trying to be grateful your friend showed up while your heart is erupting with the feeling that *there shouldn't be a reason to show up*. This shouldn't be happening. You needed more time. You have too many questions.

There is too much loss.

The people in our lives mean well. Grief is hard. And even though we all experience it, we still interact with one another awkwardly. We do not know what to say. We try to ease the pain of those we love. We want to end their heartache. And so we speak.

BEFORE YOU READ THIS NEXT PART, HEAR MY HEART: SPEAK. IF SOMEONE IS HURTING, SPEAK. SHARE ONE ANOTHER'S BURDENS. MOURN TOGETHER. ACKNOWLEDGE THEIR SUFFERING.

One of the questions I hate the most surrounding the death of my loved one continues to be, "Was she a Christian?"

I've grown up in the south. We have grown accustomed to asking questions, being neighborly, behaving hospitably to those in grief, without thinking through the *reception* of our words. In our eagerness to speak, we sometimes lose sight of the hearer.

I wonder if we would pause our inquiry if we pondered for one moment the answer may be, "no." or "I don't know."

Or with the possible shake of the head and shrug of the shoulders, "Unless the Lord saved him in his dying breath."

Or silence, thick and deafening. A lip quiver, eyes welling up, and the feeble will to hold it together.

As if I am able to hold myself together in such a moment.

And suddenly eternity has never been so abundantly clear in your mind. Death has never been so definitive. Sweet friends and family members offer condolences that are easily found in sympathy cards. They did not have the relationship with your loved one that you did. Nor the conversations you had. They did not see you on your knees in prayer. And while they will quickly share a post on social media with a cute, joyful graphic about how the Lord answers prayers - you are gut-wrenchingly aware that sometimes His answer is no.

Sometimes, the answer is that we have to go on living, unsure.

Unsure.

Sweet Sibling, the waters of uncertainty are the most painful waters I have yet to endure. If you are like me, those waters are filling your eyes now. These words are not meant to drive a stake in your heart. They are meant to reach through these pages and tell you, you are not alone. Oh, how I wish we were not unsure. How I wish we could rather answer that painful question rejoicing in *YES*.

But we must go on remembering there is hope. Because our God is in control. He holds all things together. He is good, always. He is with us. He cares for us. He is near to the broken hearted. He is making all things new.

I believe. Help my unbelief.

I will say those few sentences in every chapter. I want each of us to take these Truths to heart. We will dissect them one at a time. For now, read them. They may not be able to saturate your heart. You may not be able to absorb them right now. We will preach these Truths to ourselves. And we will do this many times through this dark night. Because, the night is long and these waves are fierce.

We will not lose sight of the Light. Even if we cannot see it.

Lord, this night is certainly long and dark. When we do not have the strength to pray, or know what words to say, please help us. When our night is filled with moaning, please help us. When we do not have the strength to ask for help, please help us. In Jesus' Name, Amen.

Of the Truths we are going to be preaching to ourselves, which Truth do you find hardest to believe right here, right now, in this moment? *(Our God is in control. He holds all things together. He is good, always. He is with us. He cares for us. He is near to the broken hearted. He is making all things new.)*

_____
_____
_____
_____
_____
_____
_____
_____
_____
_____
_____
_____
_____
_____
_____
_____
_____
_____
_____
_____
_____
_____
_____
_____
_____
_____
_____

SECOND LETTER
EULOGY

Breathe. Even if the breath is shaky, breathe.

It is okay to weep. Those sounds that come out of your body when your mourning intensifies are a kind of processing. And if we do not want to be stuck in this long night forever, we need to process.

I gave the eulogy. And this was a beautiful thing. Sharing allowed me to frame my relationship with my loved one and gift our memories to others. There were tears. There were laughs. And there was honor. There was an opportunity to make the gospel clear, the saving work done on the cross, and it was a humbling experience to speak about Jesus - knowingly being held up by Him - while literal chest pains boomed within me.

Sharing that all we have is Christ. He is all that matters in the end. He alone can save.

There is something simultaneously crushing yet heartwarming that sustains us through those initial days and weeks of loss. With so much "get up and do," we are unable to just sit and soak in the *permanence*. The *finality*. The memories flood in as a tempest, followed by the sustaining waves produced by a storm. We post on social media about the loss, check in on others impacted and grieving, share stories together as a means to lick our wounds, and operate from a place of numbness, not fully absorbing the gravity of our loss.

I believe this is grace from our Father above. One person shared with me that no tears were shed until day twenty-eight. She was so busy taking care of the needs of others through their grief, that she did not feel the floods collapse in on her until day twenty-eight. Maybe that is you. Or maybe, the dam broke for you while hearing the eulogy. Maybe you have been able to hold the waters back, afraid of the sure pain you'll let in....knowing the one you lost may not be at peace, at Home, in the arms of our Savior.

We have to walk through these waters. If we believe what we say we believe, that Jesus is the Way, the Truth, and the Life - that no one comes to the Father except through Him - or rather, if we believe what Jesus speaks (and, we do, Sweet Sibling...we believe. Help our unbelief, Lord, when what we know to be true of you hurts so deeply), then we must walk through these waters. We must ask ourselves *unbearable* questions. Is Jesus enough? Even if our loved one is not in Heaven? Is God worthy of our praise? Even if His will is stabbing right now? Does He hear us when we call, even now? Even if His answer to our many prayers for our loved one was indeed, no?

Yes. Yes. Yes. Even if. Eyes up. Don't linger on the waves. And remember, you do not have to get back to the boat on your own. Our Lord not only commands the waves. He comes *to us* on the waves.

We must go on remembering there is hope. Because our God is in control. He holds all things together. He is good, always. He is with us. He cares for us. He is near to the broken hearted. He is making all things new.

I believe. Help my unbelief.

IN THE SPACE PROVIDED, tell the Lord about your waves. Are you walking on them? Do you feel as though you are sinking? Give your heart the opportunity to pour itself out in the space provided and turn it into a prayer to the Lord.

_____

_____

_____

_____

_____

_____

_____

_____

_____

_____

_____

_____

_____

_____

_____

_____

_____

Lord, help us to believe that you will walk to us on the waves. Help us to believe that you will come to us as the waters roar. That you have been here all along, though your footprints may be unseen.

THIRD LETTER
THE STONE IS PLACED

MATTHEW 27:60 tells us Joseph rolled a great stone to the entrance of the tomb and went away.

That's what is done when stones are placed. They are placed, and *we go away*.

This is a hard letter to write. I'm praying over how it is received. I do not want to wound your heart within these pages. Crying and processing are on the way to healing, so if you have a good episode of weeping throughout this book, that may be beneficial to you in the long run. I hope so. But, I do not want to further wound you through your long night.

I'm holding your hand, figuratively, as we approach the stone. Your beloved may have a grave marker. A mausoleum or headstone. There may be no stone yet due to various circumstances. The stone will, however, be placed. And we cannot remain there. We have to walk away.

I remember, years ago, early into our marriage, going cliff jumping with my husband and younger brother. Quickly, I walked right to the edge of the cliff, counted to three, and jumped. knowing that if I did not jump at the first utterance of three, anxiety would creep in - preventing me from jumping into the waters. My husband, the wisest in our marriage, did not jump on three. He hesitated. To this day, I cannot remember if his feet ever left the cliff or not. I remember being a bit frustrated that I leapt, seemingly without fear, while he lingered.

Neither leaping nor lingering was wrong though. Both are perfectly acceptable ways to experience a day at the lake.

The stone is placed, Sweet Sibling. And you have two options in front of you. Are you going to walk away, or are you going to linger?

Standing before my loved one's casket was the most tangible reckoning I've had as I faced my inability to have one foot on earth and one foot in Heaven. I cannot take anything with me from here. I pray that the Lord uses my life to plant seeds, that He waters those seeds, and that He grows those seeds. That I will boldly proclaim Him as He opens doors for me to do so. But, I cannot cling to anyone tightly enough to get them Home with me. I cannot even cling tightly enough to Jesus to not be washed away. He has to hold me fast.

*He has to hold **me** fast.*

When His stone was placed, Joseph went away. Praise the Lord that Jesus did not do the same.

He came back.

Just as He said.

Here, at my loved one's stone, I linger. Perhaps you can

relate. Here's my dark night seen through my weak, terribly weak and shattered heart. I don't want to forget her voice, her hugs, her face. HER. I don't want to forget. And I'm afraid for the road ahead. If it ever stops hurting this much, does that mean I've stopped loving her? Does that mean I've forgotten her? I'm replaying every conversation that I ever had with her. Perhaps I misunderstood everything. Perhaps she has always known exactly who her Savior is. After all, some people live their faith out loud and others have this idea that it should be lived in quiet. Never to be spoken of.

If there truly is no sadness in Heaven, and she isn't there, does that mean my memory of her will just be gone? What was the point of God placing her in my life, to love, to cherish, to pray for, to seek His face over, for it to end like this?

This was not the ending that I prayed for. Did I not pray hard enough? Did I not present Him clearly enough? Did I, did I, did I? As if it was ever up to me.

I fool myself into thinking I was ever in control of the outcome. And right now, shattered and worn, I see all too clearly that it was never up to me. And I'm forced to ask myself unbearable questions that I cannot answer right now through this pain. The night is not only dark, but it is heavy. "The sorrow runs deep" is a phrase that could not be fully comprehended until this moment. Standing before the stone. And it is time to walk away.

I've clung for so long to an outcome I wrongfully assumed I was capable of managing. But, I could not prevent the stone from being placed.

Leaving the stone there, I went away.

Sweet Sibling, we have Jesus. He overcame death. He did not go away. He came back. And He is here for you. For me. For those of us too weak to lift our eyes to the One who is holding us fast. He knows what it is to weep. He knows what it is to have the Father turn His face away. He knows this night that you fear. And He is not leaving either of us to the clutches of this night.

We must go on remembering there is hope. Because our God is in control. He holds all things together. He is good, always. He is with us. He cares for us. He is near to the broken-hearted. He is making all things new.

I believe. Help my unbelief.

Father God, please help us as we stand here before the stone. Be gracious with us as we linger - as we claw at the stone trying to keep it from rolling in place, as if we can roll back time. This is hard and we cannot bear it. Teach us how to lay this at Your feet. We are not meant to bear this alone. The burden is too great. Help. In Jesus' Name, Amen.

Take a moment to process your grief through writing. This letter is heavy. If you need to process this letter and then write later, do. The next pages are here for you to use when and as needed.

FOURTH LETTER
HOPE UNSURE

BEFORE GOING FURTHER, no matter how long ago or how seemingly trivial given what we are discussing, write down one time when our Lord was faithful. The following pages provide space for you to do so.

WHEN MY HUSBAND WAS LITTLE, he heard someone proclaim, "if you are not 100% sure that you are saved, I am 100% sure you are not."

Sweet Sibling, if that man's words were true, then my salvation would be reliant on me. Full stop.

It would not have been possible to pull myself up out of the despair I was in. Those sounds that came out of me, the wailing, the hiding within my closet because I had come across the scent of her perfume while out grocery shopping and could not get to my closet quickly enough, and melt into a puddle on the floor, hugging my knees as tightly as I could with no consolation to be found - I could not pull myself up out of *that* despair.

But those who hope in the Lord will renew their strength. They will soar on wings like eagles. They will walk and not grow faint.

ISAIAH 40:31

How can my strength be renewed if I cannot hope in the Lord? He was and is and forever will be the only One who can save the lives of the lost. Did He just crush me? Will I ever hope again? How do I tell my children that He is good, and ask Him tomorrow on the way to school to keep them safe, when I have not the strength to even hope?

I'm going to be, perhaps, too honest with you right now. I felt manipulated. I prayed for my good, Heavenly Father to save her. He tells me to pray. He calls me to cast my cares upon Him. He commands that I trust Him. I *know* He is never wrong, He never sins. His Will is good and perfect.

But, I didn't believe it. I could not will myself to believe it. And what if I accepted that He did not save her, that I indeed, will never see her again? That she is in the place that I cannot - for the sake of your fragile heart and that of mine - even bear to write at this moment? What if I eventually accepted His Will, and one day again, by His great power and strength and mercy, I am able to praise Him fully and proclaim His goodness? What then if He takes someone else I love? Someone else who is not a believer? And I have to go through this again?

No. I cannot hope in You, my Lord...because I am afflicted in every way and positively crushed. I am perplexed, and my very soul, which You say You have saved, is indeed in despair.

How could I cling to my faith when losing someone, possibly for all eternity, caused me to question my God's very words about Himself? And how could I go to Scripture, in which I know there is life and joy and peace, when that very Scripture tells me that He wills and works according to His good pleasure?

His good pleasure.

Does this bring Him good pleasure?

Sweet Sibling, this is where we come face to face with who we are. And face to face with who God is. I will tread lightly... again, for the sake of your fragile heart and that of mine.

We are but clay in the hands of the potter. He knit us. He formed us. He called us. We are His.

Who made you? God.

What else did God make? All things.

Why did God make all things? For His glory.

You were made for His glory. You are His child. We live in a world engrossed in pain, and heartache, and sickness, and death. We have to walk in this world that our Father created. This world which once was paradise, but is now drenched in sin and death. We are ambassadors for His Kingdom. We proclaim Him loudly. We proclaim that our hope in Him is sure.

Because our Hope is. He did not promise you that He would save everyone you loved.

Christ tells us that when He said, "It is Finished," *your* salvation was secure.

He has sent us on the great commission:

...to go, make disciples of all nations, baptizing them in the Name of the Father and of the Son and of the Holy Spirit, teaching them to observe all that I have commanded you.

MATTHEW 28:19-20

And, I believe that includes us reminding each other that we can still put our hope in Him. I believe that includes us encouraging one another to recall previous examples in our own lives of His faithfulness.

And if we are so broken that we cannot see His faithfulness in our lives from times past, then we start with His faithfulness in Scripture. That book sitting beside our bed that we cannot open, but we *know*. His promise to Sarah to give her a baby, He kept. His promise to Abraham to make a nation out of him, He kept. His promise to Noah to never flood the whole earth again, He is keeping. His promise to rebuild the temple in three days, He conquered death to keep that one.

He tells us that we can hope in Him. And you may not be able to right now. Perhaps the stone has been rolled in front of you and the darkness of this tomb is all-consuming. But, that is where we lean into our fellow siblings. And we ask them to pray for us. Even if they cannot pray *with* us, we ask that they pray for us. We cannot see, so we ask them to be our sight. We cannot lift our heads, so we ask them to lift their heads. We cannot bow our knees, so we ask them to bow their knees. And we preach Truth to ourselves. Daily. Even as we cry out in agony.

We must go on remembering there is hope. Because our God is in control. He holds all things together. He is good, always. He is with us. He cares for us. He is near to the broken-hearted. He is making all things new.

I believe. Help my unbelief.

Merciful and abounding in love, Lord, help us as we walk through this valley where our heart mocks us when we hope. Please reveal to us the people in our lives to go to, and the strength and humility to ask them to pray for us. To step into this mourning with us. To bow their knees and go into this Spiritual battle with us. Be near, Father. In Jesus' Name, Amen.

·

FIFTH LETTER
GOD IS IN CONTROL

IN THE SPACE provided on the next pages, write down one time when our Lord was faithful. Allow this to be a different time than the one you wrote of in the last letter.

~

THIS IS A HARD LETTER. I tremble as I write it. This is not a letter to dive right into, throw in some Truth, and then jump out with zero thought toward your heart. I did not cherish people sharing compassionless words to me throughout my dark night; I will not do it to you.

Nevertheless, you and I both know that God is in control. We believe this. We read it in Scripture. We sing it in song. We remind others. But, if He is in control, then why?

This is a question lodged at believers over a variety of topics. It would be easier for me to sit in a coffee shop with you and have other conversations regarding His sovereignty, but that is not what brought you to this book, and it is not what brought me to write it. A specific grief brought us here. And Sweet Sibling, I do not want you to wrestle alone.

As I mentioned in the last letter, if God is in control of Sarah's baby, of the nation of Abraham, of the waters across our world, and of raising our beloved Savior from the dead, He is, indeed, in control over our lives. That breath you are taking right now, possibly through clenched teeth and agonizing heartbreak, He is in charge of it. You would not be taking it if not for Him ordaining it.

You would not love the one you lost, had He not gifted your life with the one you lost.

You would not have the memories with the one you lost, had He not gifted your life with the one you lost.

You would not be in deep agony over their eternity, had He not gifted your life with the one you lost.

Remember the time of faithfulness you wrote down earlier?

We must remember the faithfulness of our Lord. I want us to recall His faithfulness in the midst of crying out to Him, "WHY?" Let's not lose sight of the One who is faithful, just as He said, though we struggle with His sovereignty here.

If my Lord is sovereign over my next breath, He is indeed sovereign over the absence of breath.

I should not only praise Him when He answers my prayers with yes. Is He only sovereign over those who believe and not those apart from Him?

If He is only sovereign over some of us, then who is truly in control? Our Lord, or each individual person?

After those initial weeks, when friends and family moved on and the sympathies were no longer arriving in the mail, I began grief counseling. (Sweet Sibling, counseling is good. God has given us His Word, His Church, and His people. He works through His Word, His Church, and His people. Why would we not seek the counsel of those siblings He has gifted with patience, and listening, and compassion, specialized in walking with us through this very season? I know that in some church circles, counseling is frowned upon. This is to our shame, and only hurts us long-term. Do not be too prideful to seek help if/when you feel led by the Holy Spirit to do so.) So much of those first sessions were me asking again and again about His sovereignty. How could a God so loving, so compassionate, so caring of His flock, allow this to be His answer?

My counselor did what I assume all good counselors do: encouraged me to recall the times in my life that He has been faithful, acknowledged those times as being under His control, and pointed me toward Scripture. She would not point me to Scripture by suggesting that I read a certain chapter or book. She would rather ask, "are you reading your Bible?" This question was asked at every meeting. My answer for months was no. I had not been reading His Word.

I had gone from diving into Scripture, joyfully encouraging others in their Scripture reading, continually memorizing Scripture with my children, singing of His goodness and having a hunger for more of Him, to - in my weakness and sorrow - being unable to open the binding of His precious Word.

And while I know that you might be in this spot right now, I pray you will not stay here long. In fact, I am praying at this very moment, that you will pick up His Word today and read it. However many verses you are able to read right now, I pray that you do it. This will look differently for each of us walking through this dark night. In His Word, we come face to face with His sovereignty. We come face to face with the Most High. We come face to face with the One Who became sin for us. The Father turned His face away from the One who became sin that we might be with Him for all eternity.

In His Word, we come face to face with His sovereignty. "For by Him all things were created, in Heaven and on earth, visible and invisible, whether thrones or dominions or rulers or authorities - all things were created through Him and for Him." (Col. 1:16) We are created through Him and for Him. I do not want us to ignore this Truth. I was not created through Him to have my way. I was not created through Him to determine His plans. I was not created through Him to choose *His will* for Him..

I was created through Him and *for* Him.

Sweet Sibling, He created you. And this night will not last. The dawn will come. You will read that in Scripture when you are able to. You will be able to lift your hands again one day in praise to the One who is in control. You will be able to lift your voice in song (or, at least, read the lyrics without tears streaming down your face) to the One who loves you more deeply than you will ever know.

He loves you more deeply than you loved the one you lost.

The One in control of all things has not forgotten you. He has not ignored you. He has created you for a purpose. You are His workmanship. You are created in Christ Jesus. Perhaps every Sunday morning while you sit in church surrounded by people who joyfully sing "It is well with my soul," your heart screams "It is NOT well with my soul. It is not! There is no peace like a river. This sorrow puts the sea's billowing to shame. I have been taught that whatever my lot I can yet praise His Name, but I am unable to sing *It is well*. I cannot even utter a whisper of praise in this broken heart of mine."

I know. I know full well the agony within you and I weep,

even now, for your heart and how it has been crushed upon the rocks. And your heart is not crushed due to you simply missing your loved one. Your heart feels destroyed because your loved one may not have known the God who saves. And, it is too late.

Oh, Sweet Sibling. Walk with me. We must not remain here.

We must go on remembering there is hope. Because our God is in control. He holds all things together. He is good, always. He is with us. He cares for us. He is near to the broken-hearted. He is making all things new.

I believe. Help my unbelief.

Father God, I know that your Word is true. I know that You are faithful and good. I know that You are in charge of all things. I know that I am the clay and You are the potter. God, I ask that You tangibly show this child of yours that You are able to calm the storm within. I pray You remind this child that You are strong enough to handle this unbearable pain. I ask that You remind my Sweet Sibling that Your love for them is deep enough to weather the anger and hurt that they feel. Please hold us in Your hands. Hold us fast. If you do not carry us safely to shore, we will be lost among these waves. Hold us fast. Don't let us go. In Jesus' Name, Amen.

SIXTH LETTER
HE HOLDS ALL THINGS TOGETHER

He is before all things, and in Him all things hold together.

COL. 1:17

LEADING UP TO MY LOSS, I was in a Bible Study with several women studying how the Lord holds all things together - in every season. And what a wonderful study it was! We were diving deep into the Lord's Word, gaining not merely milk but good, solid meat. We were preaching the Word to ourselves and to each other, soaking His goodness deep into our hearts. We were holding one another accountable and rejoicing over what the Lord had done, was doing, and will do.

Then, one by one, we each began entering a winter season. The night became long for each of us. Work, parenting, cancer, marriage, death...a darkness washed into the lives of each of us. My beloved sisters in Christ. The Lord had been teaching us and refining us and preparing us to go into spiritual battle. And we battled together. We battled on our knees for one another. The accountability to encourage one another to be in His Word and apply Truths we were learning became an accountability *to love one another well.* Our love for one another in Christ was put into practice and tested. What good is gaining knowledge of His Word if it does not transform our lives?

When I received the devastating news, I knew who to notify. I knew the women that would battle for me. When the spiritual warfare was so tumultuous that I could not pray, I had a group of women that were already in the battle with me.

He is indeed before all things. Just as He says.

In 1 Corinthians 3, we read that Paul addressed the church of Corinth as infants - needing milk rather than meat. This does not mean that once we are further along in our Christian walk, that we no longer need milk. After all, we all need something to wash our solid food down! The Lord, in His sovereignty, knows what is to come. He knows our days ahead. He is before them. Our wonderful Father knows what we need before we do.

He knows we need milk.

He knows when we are ready for meat.

He knows we need the community of His people.

And He is not going to send us into a battle without equipping us first for what we need.

What we need is Jesus.

He knows this. He has given us Jesus. He is holding all things together in Jesus. He is holding YOU together in Jesus.

BEFORE WE GO FURTHER, **write down another example of the Lord's faithfulness in your life on the next pages.**

BEFORE THIS AGONIZING, painful, sorrow-filled season, you had milk. You knew these basic Truths of the gospel, and I dare to believe that your faith was deepening. Your love of Christ was growing. Your heart for the lost was enduring. Your desire to see His Kingdom come and spread throughout the earth was a battle cry of your soul.

Your hunger for the Lord is obvious to me because you are here. You are searching for answers to all of the whys screaming within you. You are *battling* with your grief. Your foundation upon the Rock feels like it is disappearing into sinking sand. You came into this grief with an eagerness for your lost loved one to be found in Him. You came into this grief knowing the Way, the Truth, and the Life and had been continually asking for Him to reveal Himself to more than just you. For His Kingdom to spread in the heart of your loved one. You were not merely accepting His gift of salvation to you and hiding it where none could see. You were actively asking that He would not stop with you.

When I would pray that the Lord would use my ransomed life for His glory, I also meant that through saving me, He would save my loved one. I meant that when I spoke of my Lord to her, that He would give her ears to hear. I meant that in keeping me from perishing, He would keep her from perishing too.

I meant not just me. I meant for Him to ransom her, too. I

meant for Him to not destroy me by eternally separating us. *This* was not what I meant.

In this valley, I could not eat meat. In this valley, I could not dive into another in-depth bible study. In this valley, I could not lead prayer. In this valley, I could not make it to church and remain in the service. At great risk of you closing this book and judging me as a faithless believer, recklessly writing a book to encourage fellow Christians (how dare me?!), allow me to share with you that in this valley, if not for *believing* that my children needed to be in church, I would not have gone. I would have stayed in bed on Sundays, sending my husband off to church to love the Lord, and worship Him, and teach of His goodness to others, and sing His praises without abandon, while I hid under my covers, ashamed of my doubt, my weakness, and my anger toward the One who claims to be a loving Father - a Good Father. Ashamed that part of me desired to embrace my doubt, my weakness, and my anger. My head and heart ached with the Truths I knew, but the absence of those Truths' ability to be felt.

He holds all things together?

Then why was He watching me fall apart? Furthermore, why was He allowing it?

Sweet Sibling, have you found yourself in this same valley? Longing for hope, yet despairing that there may be no hope to even search for it?

He knows the valley we find ourselves in. Not only will He meet us in the valley, but He will hold us through it.

He was not watching me fall apart. He was there holding

me together. He *is* before all things. He was in my days leading up to the valley of the shadow of death. He was fully orchestrating the season which preceded my winter.

In the valley, I could not feel Him. I could not see Him. I could not hear Him.

But, He never commanded that I know exactly what He is doing - nor *why* He is doing.

He commanded that I have faith.

And when I couldn't, He held me fast. As He is holding you fast now. When He said, "it is finished," He did not leave us alone to survive in this valley. Our lives in Him were promised, regardless of our ability to eat meat or merely drink milk. He promised to lead us through the valley of the shadow of death. He promised to be with us. Our doubt, our weakness, and our anger do not determine if our God remains a promise-keeper.

He is a promise-keeper. He has always been. He will always be. He knows your days and has been preparing and leading you to where you are. He is holding you together now and will remain with you. He is holding you fast, and Sweet Sibling, if all you can do is drink milk - the meat will be there for another day. This season will not last forever.

We must go on remembering there is hope. Because our God is in control. He holds all things together. He is good, always. He is with us. He cares for us. He is near to the broken- hearted. He is making all things new.

I believe. Help my unbelief.

God, hold us together. Hold me together. Thank you for not leaving us in this valley to merely survive another day. Thank you that you give us both milk and meat. Help us to receive that which You give us. In Jesus' Name, Amen.

SEVENTH LETTER
HE IS GOOD, ALWAYS

MARK 10:18 tells us that "no one is good except God alone." We find in Psalm 145:9 that "the Lord is good to all, and His tender mercies are over all His works.

Here, in this season, these two Truths feel like monstrous waves crashing in on us. No one is good but God. And over all His works, including this darkened valley where we languish, His tender mercies are woven as a covering.

Let's have a moment to address our uncertainty. Sweet Sibling, to be clear, we do not know where our loved ones are spending eternity. Only God knows. God, in His great mercy, may have saved our loved ones in their final breath. I want us not to ignore the possibility of them calling out to Jesus in that final moment in repentance and faith. We do not know. We mourn, grieved to our core, but we do not get the final say. He does. Praise the Lord.

Perhaps your lost loved one, by human standards, was evil.

Perhaps your lost loved one, by human standards, was a saint.

Neither matter, Sweet Sibling.

The Lord is good. He alone. And we cannot earn our salvation. It is a free gift from God alone. We must understand, affirm, and believe that He alone is good before we accept that He is good *always*.

In the space provided on the next page, write an example of His goodness in your life.

Now, write an example of when, in His goodness, He withheld something from you:

_____

_____

_____

_____

_____

_____

_____

_____

_____

_____

_____

_____

_____

_____

_____

_____

_____

_____

That second writing prompt may have been difficult for you. Often, I find it easy to acknowledge His blessings, His goodness, His gifts that are a direct "yes" to a prayer I've submitted to Him. It is a bit more difficult to see His goodness immediately upon receiving the answer of "no." Yet, even when His response is to withhold, He is good. *Always.*

Remember that we must first understand He alone is good, before we can believe that He is good always. He alone is good. As my sorrow gave way to more anger, I began elevating my loved one to a place of salvation being 'earnable.' I began asking the Lord, with frustration rising, how He could keep from saving her. She was *good.* And in my questioning of His will, in my confusion and sorrow and aching for her soul, I traded what He alone defines as good for what I alone determined was good.

And here is where we must walk this valley with caution. With fear and trembling now, I approach this topic.

The Lord, in His goodness, is still a Promise-Keeper even when my faith is wavering. He is still holding me fast even when my heart is tempted to run away as a prodigal once more. But, that does not give me clearance to tell the King of Kings how He should rule His Kingdom. I have never approached the Lord with more fear and trembling than I did while in the valley. Fear and trembling was my covering. What I *knew* to be true and what I could *believe* to be true and what I *wanted* to be true were in constant turmoil. And I believe, in the Lord's constant goodness and compassion for us, that He not only knows we are in turmoil and cares deeply, but that He also calls us to place our fears and heartache in His hands. He does not command us to languish alone. He does not forsake us when we have questions. He does not belittle us when we should be eating meat, but in our humanity can barely stomach the milk of His Word.

The Lord knows we want to see the best in those we love. We, however, do not determine their *goodness*. We do not declare our loved ones pure. We do not clothe our loved ones in righteousness.

Christ does.

And when we stand before the throne, either are covered by the blood of the Lamb, or we are not.

Either Christ has clothed us in His righteousness, or we are undone.

Each of us can look over our own lives and see our own unworthiness. I can look into my yesterday and see there where I nailed my Savior to the cross.

And, if you are honest....so can you.

But, in His goodness, He did not leave us on the hillside undelivered. He alone is good. He alone can perform such goodness. He alone is good, always. And that goodness, we cling to. That deliverance, we cling to. That saving grace, which we ache to be given to all, we trust the Lord's will in gifting.

We must go on remembering there is hope. Because our God is in control. He holds all things together. He is good, always. He is with us. He cares for us. He is near to the broken-hearted. He is making all things new.

I believe. Help my unbelief.

Our Good Father, thank you for not leaving us undelivered on the hillside. Thank you that You are good. Please give us the strength to see Your goodness, Your deliverance, Your saving grace which is Yours to give. Let our hearts continue to ache for the lost in this world while also causing us to rejoice in what You have already done. You are good. Help us to believe You are good always. In Jesus' Name, Amen.

EIGHTH LETTER
HE IS WITH YOU

Fear not, for I have redeemed you; I have called you by name, you are mine. When you pass through the waters, I will be with you; and through the rivers, they shall not overwhelm you; when you walk through fire you shall not be burned, and the flame shall not consume you.

ISAIAH 43:1B-2

WHEN YOU READ THIS VERSE, what thoughts come to mind? Do you believe that He is with you, that He will not let you be overwhelmed, that you will not be burned nor consumed? Why or why not?

THIS LETTER, Sweet Sibling, I pray you are able to receive with hope and assurance in your heart. After all, it is not my promise. It is His promise. He is the Light in the darkness. The night has been so long. Perhaps it has been quite a while since you were able to look up and glimpse the Light; even so, look up. He is indeed with you now.

There is a peace that may be starting to roll in. *Let it.* The crushing waves of sorrow can be deafening and far more excruciating than we ever could have imagined. But, in time, waves of peace will come in these treacherous waters. If your response is similar to what mine was, perhaps you want to try to swim away from the peaceful rumblings entering your grief-stricken soul. There is a darkness so intense that in my humanity I had not the strength to reach out and swim toward the peaceful tide. I knew the waves offering hope were there, threatening to break through the walls that I had allowed around my heart. It took time before I was able to rest and see that the waters were stilling.

That He was stilling them. Just as He said He could.

The Lord had a covering over me. His tender mercies covered me. And as more peaceful waves broke on the horizon, I began to not only trust that the Light could see me....I could trust that the Light was with me. And as He slowly, gently, compassionately rolled peaceful waters over my walls, my pain and grief began to diminish. It was tangibly still there and thick. But now it was malleable. His peaceful waters were being added to the clay that is me. The Potter, moistening my anger, my fear, my heartache, was beginning to wipe away my tears. He was with me. He was *with* me in this valley. He did not put me here and leave. He was not testing me to see if I could claw my way out on my own. He already knew I could not.

He never left. I could not see Him for so long. Yet, He was here. Those waves of peace that I pushed away at first were real. And my God would not relent now.

He had not forsaken me.

He had not given up on me in my doubt.

He had not turned His back on me to succumb to the roaring waves.

He had not grown weary of holding me fast.

No, Sweet Sibling. He pursued me through gentle, faithful waves.

He is in control, just as He said. He is holding all things together, just as He said. He is good, just as He said. And now, He is with me, just as He said. I can see that He never left.

It is the Lord Who goes before you. He will be with you; He will not leave you or forsake you. Do not fear or be dismayed.

DEUTERONOMY 31:8

Sweet Sibling, the sun is dawning. He is with you upon the waves. He is with you in the valley. He is with you in the fire. You are not alone in your grief. You never were. He is where you are. And though you may not *feel* His presence at all times, your feelings do not speak for the King of Kings and Lord of Lords. He has told you exactly where He will be. And He is a Promise Keeper. He is faithful, always. And He has been holding you fast. Just as He said He would.

We must go on remembering there is hope. Because our God is in control. He holds all things together. He is good, always. He is with us. He cares for us. He is near to the broken-hearted. He is making all things new.

I believe. Help my unbelief.

Mighty God, the One Who stills the waters, thank You that You do not forsake Your children. Thank You that You do not give up on us in our doubt. You hold back the roaring waves so that we do not succumb to it. And though we are weary, You will never grow weary of holding us fast. Please, do not let us go. In Jesus' Name, Amen.

NINTH LETTER
HE CARES FOR US

WHILE IN THE VALLEY, I could pray for others. I believed the Lord cared for them. I believed that He would hear my prayers when I lifted up a brother or sister in need, no matter their need. When others were grieving and needed comfort - I believed He would hear me when I called upon Him, and that He cared.

However, I could not pray for myself. I believed a lie that He did not care for me. I am not sure exactly when this lie crept in; but, crept in, it did. And it took root. And the lie began weaving itself into the way I thought and felt.

As the war raged within my heart and mind, the spiritual warfare was undeniable. I knew what I knew to be true. Oh, but strength to believe what I knew to be true was a cry I had not the strength to pray. I felt that I was slipping off of my foundation. I questioned if my foundation truly was ever upon the Rock; after all, don't we sing that on Christ the solid Rock we stand while all other ground is sinking sand? Why was I sinking if my foundation was the Rock? *How* was I sinking if I truly belonged to His Kingdom?

Was it possible to have a foundation on the Rock while simultaneously being incapable of standing?

As my feet were seemingly sinking into sand, or rather, as the current was seemingly pulling me off of the Rock, God was graciously leading me to pray. My grief did not keep those around me from needing His intervention in their lives and circumstances. My grief did not keep those around me from asking for prayer.

I could not pray for myself, *yet*. But, I could pray for those around me.

Do you know what happens when you pray for others? Your heart is reminded of Who you are praying to. Your heart is reminded of why you are praying to Him. Your heart is reminded of what He is capable of. Your heart, praise God, is redirected to Him. You see His hands holding this world. You see Him hold those you care for.

As the Lord graciously brought me back to prayer, He began leading me to His Word again. How could I pray that He would care for others, without being reminded of His Word telling me He cares for me? How could I pray that His will be done, without being reminded of His Word telling me His will is best? How could I pray that forgiveness would abound after wrongdoing, without being reminded of His Word telling me that He forgives? How could I pray for prodigals to come home, without being reminded of His Word telling me that He welcomes prodigals?

Do you see what our God was doing? He was gently and

graciously bringing me face to face with His Truth. The lies that had threatened to take deeper root had no choice but to be uprooted. And this was not my doing. Our Father was pruning the lies as He revealed in His Word what is True. Alive and moving, His Word was breathing life into the valley I found myself in. He preached to my heart through the prayers He led me to pray for others.

And He revealed, once again, that He was fighting for me. Because He cares for me. Just as He said.

The Lord will fight for you; you need only to be still.

EXODUS 14:14

And what good news is this. Grief is so burdensome that it taxes us physically. Emotionally. Mentally. And as we have found, sometimes it taxes us spiritually. It is good news to read that the fighting is not for us to do.

I have long loved this verse. It was a battle cry of my heart during multiple seasons of my life. And the Lord has always been faithful to prove He will fight. In other seasons, my being still did not come naturally. That, in and of itself, was a battle for me. During grief...during *this* grief...being still wasn't a choice. I was too taxed. Too weak. Too stricken. I could not fight for myself, for my faith, or for my heart. I was in deep mourning over the unknown of my loved one's soul, and its resting place.

Being still wasn't a choice. It was the only possibility.

Clawing our own way out of the valley is not a choice. There is only one Way.

Creating light in the darkness is not a choice. There is only one Light.

And that one Way - that one Light - not only cares for you; He is fighting for you.

We know the Scriptures.

Cast your anxiety upon Him.

1 PETER 1:7

God is mindful of and cares for us.

PSALMS 8:4

We are of more value than the sparrows.

MATT. 10:29-31

We can hear certain verses rattled off with such frequency that we may forget His Word is alive and moving. Hear this, Sweet Sibling. His Word is alive and moving. And it will not return void. Today, I want you to read and receive that He cares for you. He is actively choosing to care for you.

We can cast our anxieties upon Him because He does care for us. To cast our anxieties is not a passive action. It is a practice. And every time we practice laying our burdens at His feet, He will prove Himself faithful. I know and understand that coming out of this valley, *feeling* His care may be different for each of us. Please remember that our feelings do not define who God is. God defines who He is. This is all the more reason for us to practice casting our anxieties upon Him. As we trust Him with our burdens, regardless of our feelings, He will prove His care and faithfulness.

He does care for us, and He is fighting for us. Just as He says.

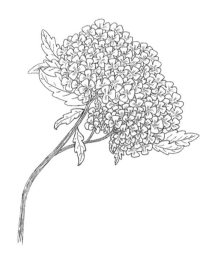

God being mindful of us is not passive. It is a continual choice. It is characteristic of who He is. It is love in action. He not only knows of every sparrow that falls to the ground, but He knows every hair upon your head. And He is purposefully mindful of *you*. Oh, Sweet Sibling, how mindful our Father is of you! In this valley, in this shadow of death, in this storm, I pray you find these verses proving His faithfulness in your life.

IN THE SPACE provided on the next pages, write an example of when the Lord has cared for you.

EMMIE SEALS

~

IN THE SPACE PROVIDED, write an example of when the Lord
has cared for someone in your life:

_____

_____

_____

_____

_____

_____

_____

_____

_____

_____

_____

_____

_____

_____

_____

_____

_____

Sweet Sibling, you will find in Scripture that you are not the first to go through grief. You are not the first child of God to be in despair and be found pleading with Him. "How long, O Lord?" is not a cry held only by you. Think of the prophets. Read through the prophets in the Old Testament.

You are not the first to cry these words while praying for a loved one's salvation. You are not the first to cry it while praying the breaking of your heart would cease. You are not the first to find yourself on the Rock, and realize that you are too weak to keep yourself there. And you will not be the last to find that a compassionate Father will hold His children fast - even though they beat against His bosom crying for a different outcome.

The prophets, in their sufferings and in their cries to the Lord, found a loving Father who was working in the lives of His people *for* His people, who was near to the broken-hearted, and who remained long-suffering with their questions and struggles. His actions were not always the ones they wanted Him to take. However, His actions have always been filled with an abundance of care and concern for His church. He has always been fighting for His people.

And He is fighting for us.

He is fighting for you.

Sweet Sibling, He is proving that He still cares, and always will care, for you.

We must go on remembering there is hope. Because our God is in control. He holds all things together. He is good, always. He is with us. He cares for us. He is near to the broken- hearted. He is making all things new.

I believe. Help my unbelief.

Loving Lord, how long? How long will we ache? And yet, we know that You care about this very heartache. You care and You are fighting for us. You care and You are actively mindful of us. Lord, please do not stop proving to us that You care. Please do not stop showing us in Your Word that You care. In our weakness, we need You to remind us, to keep our eyes on You, to burn the lies that threaten to sow roots. Please be ever present, ever near. In Jesus' Name, Amen.

TENTH LETTER

HE IS NEAR TO THE BROKENHEARTED

The Lord is near to the brokenhearted and saves the crushed in spirit.

PSALM 34:18

I HAVE a letter board with this reminder on it. I placed the letters of this verse upon the sign and set it on top of the chest of drawers in the bedroom shortly before my loved one passed. This verse was on my heart in the weeks prior. I had been pondering it for a different reason.

As I looked at it with blurry, sore, tear-stung eyes in the days that followed my loved one's death, it seemed to mock me.

My Lord did not feel near.

My spirit was crushed and being saved seemed laughable. Like Sarai, I didn't trust His promise.

And it wasn't my spirit that needed saving from this crushing blow, was it? I ached with an ache that you know too well. An ache that could not be bandaged with mere words meant to comfort.

No. This was an ache of eternal significance. And my Lord was the only One with the power to comfort my broken heart. He was also the only One with the power to have stopped my heart from breaking if He had chosen to do so.

My soul was wrecked upon the rocks of the Lighthouse. The very One who would lead me Home, the very One who saved me from eternal separation from Him, had possibly eternally separated me from her.

There is a desperation lodged in our throats knowing we are not eternally separated from our Father, yet finding ourselves blazingly aware of eternity. A desperation that grows with intense urgency. This earth is not our home. And we must not go Home alone! The harvest is plentiful, but the laborers are few. Oh, Lord, let me labor! Rewind the time. Let me labor more for You. For the sake of my loved one, please let me labor more.

As I found myself here, clawing my way down the rocks in desperation to save my loved one already gone, there were gentle, consistent whispers from the Spirit beckoning me to find comfort in the Man of sorrows, in the One acquainted with grief. The Spirit was reminding me that I do not get the final say; the Spirit was reminding me of the thief on the cross and that I know not the final moments of a person's life; the Spirit was reminding me that God is good, always, and I could trust Him with my slain heart. Though I could not feel Him near nor could I feel my crushed spirit being saved, He was right there. And my spirit, He had already saved.

Everywhere I would be, He had already been there.

Perhaps Jesus did not claw His way down from Heaven, but He did come down desperate to save His beloved sheep that were lost. If He didn't save, His beloved sheep would never make it to the Lighthouse. If He didn't save, His beloved sheep would indeed be crushed. And would not be *allowed* near.

Sweet Sibling, once upon a time we were not allowed

near. Once upon a time, our broken heart would have remained broken.

But, He promised us a different story.

In the space provided in the next pages, I invite you to confess to the Lord your broken heart. He already knows. I encourage you to invite Him into the brokenness. Take your time. I am praying now that as you write, you see that He is already there.

Now, in the space provided, I encourage you to confess your fears and doubts. Turn these fears and doubts over to the one who longs to heal your crushed spirit.

_____

_____

_____

_____

_____

_____

_____

_____

_____

_____

_____

_____

_____

_____

_____

_____

_____

_____

YOU HAVE BEEN on the battlefield while in this valley. You cannot see your enemy, but you have, no doubt, been fraught with fears and doubts that Satan has tried to turn into lies which you would believe and hold fast. We are taught in 1 Peter 5 that the Devil prowls about as a roaring lion. He does not sympathize that you are weak from mourning. He rejoices in it. There is a sadness that seems to have pierced your very soul, and the Devil has leapt into that pain to make it his home.

Sweet Sibling, we are told to be watchful. To be mindful. This is me pointing you to Jesus and reminding you to be watchful. To be mindful of what our adversary is trying to do.

Just as Satan believed he had won when our Savior was slain and the stone was rolled in front of the tomb, he believes now that he can sow fear and doubt into the soil of your soul and win.

He cannot.

Rise up, Sweet Sibling. Our Lord has already won! It is time to divert your eyes from the waves crashing on the shore and to the Lighthouse on which you stand. He is near. Oh, Sweet Sibling He is near! He has always been right here. He never left you. He came down for you while you were lost, long before you took your first earthly breath. He saw you then, He knew your broken heart was in need of a Savior and not only did He save you while you were still a sinner - He

97

promised to be with you always. And He is faithful. He has been holding you fast all along. Your spirit has been crushed. But you have not been destroyed.

The night has been long, and it is not yet over. There are still waves ahead that will threaten to push you off of the Rock. Take heart - though you may feel weak and unstable, you cannot be moved. Our God has you.

I pray that you are more clearly seeing that which you may have been unable to see when you first opened this book.

Because this milk we have been drinking together is nourishing. I pray it is seeping into the crevices of your valley and refreshing your soul.

We must go on remembering there is hope. Because our God is in control. He holds all things together. He is good, always. He is with us. He cares for us. He is near to the broken- hearted. He is making all things new.

I believe. Help my unbelief.

Providing Lord, You are the Good Shepherd. Please keep nourishing us. Sow HOPE in You and Lord, even joy, into our broken hearts. You are able to heal. To restore. To refresh. Please lead us beside still waters. Let our cups run over. Let us rejoice in You and sing that our hearts have been made glad. Heal, we pray. In Jesus' Name, Amen.

ELEVENTH LETTER

HE IS MAKING ALL THINGS NEW

Behold, I am doing a new thing; now it springs forth, do you not perceive it? I will make a way in the wilderness and rivers in the desert.

ISAIAH 43:19

ON THE NEXT PAGES, give an example of when Satan meant evil for something in your life or in the life of another, and God used it for good.

Do you believe there is anything too dark, too painful, too impossible for the Lord to use it and mold it into something good?

_____

_____

_____

_____

_____

_____

_____

_____

_____

_____

_____

_____

_____

_____

_____

_____

_____

_____

And I heard a loud voice from the throne saying, 'Behold, the dwelling place of God is with man. He will dwell with them, and they will be His people, and God Himself will be with them as their God. He will wipe away every tear from their eyes, and death shall be no more, neither shall there be mourning, nor crying, nor pain anymore, for the former things have passed away.' And He Who was seated on the throne said, 'Behold, I am making all things new.' Also He said, 'Write this down, for these words are trustworthy and true.' And He said to me, 'It is done! I am the Alpha and the Omega, the beginning and the end. To the thirsty I will give from the spring of the water of life without payment.'

REVELATION 21:3-6

Part of me wants to just stop and end this book with that.

However, I know that you may be reading this at a time when you are unable to believe that your tears will actually be wiped away one day, and that He will indeed make all things new, and that He will give to the thirsty, even when - no, especially when - the thirsty doubts.

Re-read the first half of Isaiah 43:19. Our all knowing, gracious Father not only tells us exactly what He is doing -

doing a new thing - He also is mindful of our human-ness and asks a question: "do you not perceive it?" We are not God. He knew then and He knows now that we may not perceive what He is doing. Who can discern how He is willing and working at every turn?

Yet, He is.

Whether or not we perceive it, He is working. And He is doing a new thing.

Not only a new thing. He has made a way in the wilderness and rivers in the desert.

Rivers in the desert.

Sweet Sibling, I was so incredibly parched in my darkest days of doubt and fear and anguish. Whatever He was giving to quench my thirst then, I had no consciousness of. But not being able to perceive Him or His work does not negate His Word. When my feelings and perceptions do not line up with His Word, it is not His Word that I should question. It is my feelings and perceptions that need questioning.

I'm wondering if, like mine, your valley is lined with perceptions and feelings bleeding from your heart, pushing back against the Truth we know because it is not the Truth we feel? One verse that echoed again and again in my mind throughout this valley of grief was Jeremiah 17:9:

The heart is deceitful above all things, and desperately sick; who can understand it?

JEREMIAH 17:9

My heart was desperately sick.

Desperately sick.

I knew that it was sick. It was sick with grave eternal significance. The desperation for the unknown and the *feeling* of utter hopelessness. Praise God that I knew my heart was sick. I knew it was so desperate that it would deceive. Any knowledge of my heart's sickness was not my wisdom at all, however. I know it was the Holy Spirit at work within me, holding the sickness back even when I *felt* surrounded and overcome by it.

The Holy Spirit was a steady stream in my desert, giving

unto me the stream of the water of life (Rev. 21:6) even though I still *felt* thirst.

I did not *feel* hope.

I did not *feel* that God is in control - and worse if He was, I didn't *feel* I could trust Him.

I did not *feel* Him holding all things together. No, I *felt* like I was falling apart.

I did not *feel* He is good, always.

I did not *feel* Him with me.

I did not *feel* His care of me.

I did not *feel* His nearness to my broken-heart.

I did, however, *feel* something new: absence from Him, darkness with no hope for Light, loss of my footing upon the Rock, loss of any grip, and grave eternal significance.

I absolutely *felt*. By God's mercy, He held me fast, just as He is holding you fast now, despite what I felt.

His promises are not mine to bring to fruition.

They are His. And His alone.

I want to say that again. His promises are not ours to bring to fruition. The work He is doing in our lives is not ours to complete. Christ completes His work in us. All of God's promises are fulfilled in Christ. Christ is our hope and it is not our doing to make Him so. It is His. Sweet Sibling, all of those emotions we feel at war within us are a rushing tide trying to force us to control that which we cannot.

This is not ours to control. This grief, this sorrow, this night is not ours to survive. We are not meant to 'pull ourselves up by our bootstraps' and sweep this grief under the rug.

No, Sweet Sibling. This is His to control. This grief, this sorrow, this night is His to carry us through. We are not pulling ourselves up or sweeping away anything. He is walking with us, fighting for us, making a way in the wilderness and rivers in the desert, and He is making all things new.

Can you not perceive it?

The sorrow runs deep. But our God says the dawn is coming.

The tears flood as waves. But our God says He will wipe every tear away.

But the other rebuked him, saying, 'Do you not fear God, since you are under the same sentence of condemnation? And we indeed justly, for we are receiving the due reward of our deeds; but this man has done nothing wrong.' And he said, 'Jesus, remember me when you come into your kingdom.' And He said to him, 'Truly, I say to you, today you will be with me in paradise.'

LUKE 23:40-43

Sweet Sibling, I do not *know* where my loved one is. You do not *know* where yours is. And no matter what we *feel*, we believe that the Lord gets final say. He is in control. And if the thief upon the cross repented, believed, and was saved during his final moments, wouldn't our Lord be faithful to save our loved ones if they repented and believed in their hearts in their final moments?

"He will wipe away every tear from their eyes, and death shall be no more, neither shall there be mourning, nor crying, nor pain anymore, for the former things have passed away.'

And He Who was seated on the throne said, 'Behold, I am making all things new.'" (Revelation 21:4-5a)

Sweet Sibling, you will not be here forever. Look up. He has already carried you through so much of this valley.. It is not my promise to keep. It is His. But I will repeat it until my dying breath: He is making all things new.

There is hope. Our God is in control. He holds all things together. He is good, always. He is with us. He cares for us. He is near to the broken-hearted. He is making all things new.

I believe.

Dear good and gracious Father, thank you for not leaving me in my fear and doubt. Thank you for not letting me go when my belief was failing. Thank you that I do not have to hold onto you, for I am too weak. Thank you for holding onto me. Thank you for fighting for me when I was too weak, too pained, too angry to even ask for help. Thank you for continuing to bring your Word into my heart, for preaching Truth to me when it was hard to hear and receive it, and for proving again that You are good. Even in this unknown, You are still good. In Jesus' Name, Amen.

SINCERELY

HERE IN SCRIPTURE, we are reminded that we are not alone. Asaph cries out to the Lord with a longing to remember his song in the night. Yet, he moans when he remembers God. He asks if the Lord will ever be favorable again. He wonders if the Lord has forgotten to be gracious.

Sweet Sibling, the Lord will not forsake you. We find in Scripture that these questions and searchings will not cast you away from His presence. Instead, we will indeed be reminded of His faithfulness and seek to recall it again and again. We are reminded that though His footprints may be unseen, He is with us.

PSALM 77
In the Day of Trouble I Seek the Lord
To the choirmaster: according to Jeduthun. A Psalm of Asaph.

¹I cry aloud to God,
aloud to God, and he will hear me.
² In the day of my trouble I seek the Lord;
in the night my hand is stretched out without
    wearying;
my soul refuses to be comforted.

³ When I remember God, I moan;
when I meditate, my spirit faints. Selah
⁴ You hold my eyelids open;
I am so troubled that I cannot speak.
⁵ I consider the days of old,
the years long ago.
⁶ I said,¹ "Let me remember my song in the night;
let me meditate in my heart."
Then my spirit made a diligent search:
⁷ "Will the Lord spurn forever,
and never again be favorable?
⁸ Has his steadfast love forever ceased?
Are his promises at an end for all time?
⁹ Has God forgotten to be gracious?
Has he in anger shut up his compassion?" Selah
¹⁰ Then I said, "I will appeal to this,
to the years of the right hand of the Most High."
¹¹ I will remember the deeds of the LORD;
yes, I will remember your wonders of old.
¹² I will ponder all your work,
and meditate on your mighty deeds.
¹³ Your way, O God, is holy.
What god is great like our God?
¹⁴ You are the God who works wonders;
you have made known your might among the
    peoples.
¹⁵ You with your arm redeemed your people,
the children of Jacob and Joseph. Selah

¹⁶ When the waters saw you, O God,
when the waters saw you, they were afraid;
indeed, the deep trembled.
¹⁷ The clouds poured out water;
the skies gave forth thunder;
your arrows flashed on every side.
¹⁸ The crash of your thunder was in the whirlwind;
your lightnings lighted up the world;
the earth trembled and shook.
¹⁹ Your way was through the sea,
your path through the great waters;
yet your footprints were unseen.
²⁰ You led your people like a flock
by the hand of Moses and Aaron.

SUGGESTED SONGLIST FOR YOUR HEART

- Weary Traveler by Jordan St. Cyr
- All I Have is Christ by Sovereign Grace Music
- Be Still My Soul by Lisbeth Scott
- Consider the Stars by Keith and Kristyn Getty
- The Commission by Cain
- Though He Slays Me by Shane and Shane
- Abide by Aaron Keyes
- It is Well with My Soul by Audrey Assad
- In Christ Alone by Keith and Kristyn Getty
- Give me Jesus by Fernando Ortega
- The Lord is My Salvation by Keith and Kristyn Getty
- Praise You in this Storm by Casting Crowns
- In Jesus' Name by Katy Nicole
- Undone by Sovereign Grace Music

ACKNOWLEDGMENTS

I am deeply humbled as I sit here and consider the deep and wide community the Lord has given me through the darkest season of my life. I am one that tends to jump head first into things, and yet I know that if I do that here, I will inevitably leave people off of the list. That is not my desire. There is a reason why I have kept from writing this. However, a sincere thank you is meant to be said to so many.

To my Grief Counselor: you asked me if I process through writing. I laughed, and then I cried, as I shared with you my love for writing and yet, my inability to do so in the current season. You continually and gently pointed me to Scripture, to my Savior, and encouraged me to write. The Lord nudged me through you and I am grateful to you for being used as an empty vessel to pour into me.

To my friend, Angela: you have suffered so much in your life and yet you do not allow bitterness to take root. You step into the dark valley with those in your life who are grieving, ready and willing to have your heart broken so that your friends *know* they are not alone. I want to be more like you. You wept with me. You prayed for me. You did not try to 'fix' the hurt but rather displayed the calling in Scripture: "mourn with those who mourn." Thank you for mourning with me.

To my friend and editor, Beth: When my earth quaked, I texted you, "I don't know how to do this." You did. You knew exactly what to say, how to say it, when to say it, and you have not once ceased to push me toward healing - toward Jesus. I thank you. Thank you for being the first to read (and critique) this raw, outpouring of my grief. Thank you for encouraging me to write. Thank you for being a safe place to share such doubt and vulnerability that we too often hide from the church. You are a good friend. And I love you.

To Cherise, Cachaca, Cyndi, Chavela, Breanne, Katie: You ladies were the first to know my agony and your prayers rose up immediately and often. The Lord placed you all in my life, and I dare say "for such a time as this." I am eternally grateful to each of you. May we remind each other continually that He is with us in every season.

To Momzi: You are a confidant, a friend, a godly example in every interaction. You have held my heart in your prayers. When together, I have not ever felt the need to wear a mask. You are a beautiful gift from the Lord in my life. Please, never doubt my love for you. I am so grateful to God above for giving me you.

To my Mommy: You held my hand. You gave me space to grieve. You listened even when it was painful. You encouraged me. You spoke Truth into my life. You displayed grace and granted me the opportunity to break - which was necessary to get onto this road to healing. I love you. I am for you. I see you. There is brokenness in our lineage. Praise the Lord! His mercies are more. Thank you for continually reminding me of His love.

To my Church Home: You never shy away from preaching and practicing Truth. You are a safe place to worship even when the song cannot be sung out loud. Even when the tears burn. From the Word preached, to the songs sung, to the prayers lifted, to the people living life together, you display the Psalms. There is worship in lament. There is worship in thanksgiving. And both give the Lord glory. Thank you for making space for those in dark valleys. We do not have to put on a show or 'tidy up' to be welcome in our church building, or to be welcomed by our Redeemer.

To my Children: I love you. Some of you brought me a kleenex. Some of you wiped my tears. Some of you gave me random hugs. One of you instinctively knew during different moments and those instincts led to you reaching out and squeezing my hand. You each loved me well through this season and I hope that I loved you well through your questions. I only ever sought to point you to Jesus. I pray that He uses the darkness from this season to shine all the more brightly in your eyes. He is worthy of your trust. Of your hope. Of your faith. Seek Him, my darlings.

To my Husband: Not once did you make me feel anything other than your Sister in Christ, even through my questioning. Even through my doubt and fear and anger. I need you to read and see this. You treated me so well throughout this valley. Thank you. I shared with you my deepest, and darkest moments, and you did not shy away. You entered into them with me. When you didn't think it wise to speak out loud, you held your tongue and I know you prayed in silence. When you thought it wise to speak out loud, you did so with gentleness, kindness, and support. I am so grateful to you. God gave me a wonderful husband and you, daily, strive to fulfill that role in a manner worthy of the calling. Thank you for not leaving me to weep alone. Thank you for loving those I love. Thank you for allowing your heart to be broken when mine is broken. Here's to continued healing. I love you.

To My Savior: You are in control. You hold all things together. You are good, always. You are with me. You care for me. You are near to my broken heart. You are making all things new. I thought my voice would never rise again—never believe the hope and mercy and love it proclaimed. But, you restored my soul. I praise You. You did not leave me. You did not forsake me. You have given me back my song in the night. I praise You. Hallelujah.

ABOUT THE AUTHOR

Emmie Seals was born and raised in the hills of Tennessee where she still resides with her husband, four children, dog, and four rabbits. She is passionate about literacy and creating works that can act as mirrors and windows into the lives of others, cultivating empathy, compassion, and in her work, *A Different Kind of Grief*, specifically pointing others to the One who is ever faithful. When not writing, you can find her engaging in her community through local events, on the PTO Board, volunteering in her church, engaging with local schools and libraries, or snuggled up with her children for quality story time. Her writings are a warm embrace that touch the heart strings with each read and echo to readers that they are not alone.

Visit her website at **breakthesealpublishing.com**